Watch It Grow
Spider
Barrie Watts

W
FRANKLIN WATTS
LONDON • SYDNEY

First published in 2004 by Franklin Watts
96 Leonard Street, London EC2A 4XD

Franklin Watts Australia
45-51 Huntley Street, Alexandria, NSW 2015

© Barrie Watts 2004

Editor: Kate Newport
Art director: Jonathan Hair
Photographer: Barrie Watts
Illustrator: David Burroughs

The author would like to thank Mark Pennell, Ray Gabriel and
Andy Matthews for their invaluable help and assistance in the
preparation of this book.

A CIP catalogue record for this book
is available from the British Library

ISBN 0 7496 5430 9

Printed in Hong Kong, China

How to use this book

Watch It Grow has been specially designed to cater for a range
of reading and learning abilities. Initially children may just
follow the pictures. Ask them to describe in their own words
what they see. Other children will enjoy reading the single
sentence in large type, in conjunction with the pictures. This
single sentence is then expanded in the main text. More adept
readers will be able to follow the text and pictures by
themselves through to the conclusion of the life cycle.
Note: Although a tarantula spider is featured in this book, it is
not typical of the growth and behaviour of all types of spider.

Contents

Spiders come from eggs.

This is a large female tarantula spider. She lays over 400 eggs and wraps them in an **egg sac**.

The egg sac is made of silk. Spiders spin lengths of fine silk, using **spinnerets** at the rear of their bodies. The silk is wrapped round and round the bundle of eggs.

The female spider looks after the eggs.

These tarantula eggs are as big as a pinhead. Inside each one, a baby spider is growing. The female tarantula carries the **egg sac** with her sharp **fangs**.

She keeps the eggs warm and
protects them from **predators**. The
female turns the sac around many
times each day to mix the eggs up.
This allows each egg to get
warmth from her body. The eggs
need warmth to survive.

The eggs hatch.

After four weeks, the eggs begin to change. The shell becomes soft and thin, and the shape of the baby spider shows through. Soon they are ready to hatch. The tiny spiders push their way out of the shell, into the **egg sac**. Newly-hatched **spiderlings** are called **nymphs**. They have no eyes or hairs. They do not look like adult spiders.

The nymphs stay in the egg sac.

The silk thread of the **egg sac** is very strong and protects the **nymphs** from **predators**, including other spiders. It also helps to keep them warm. Their bodies and mouths are still soft so they cannot eat. They live on the food which they ate in the egg. After two weeks they shed their skin. They now have tiny eyes.

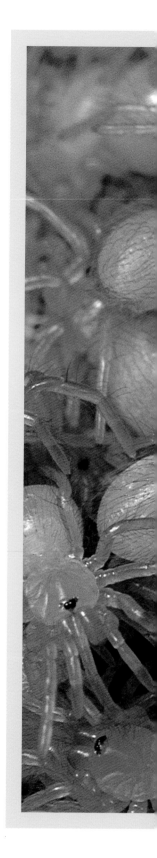

The baby spiders leave the egg sac.

Two weeks later, the **nymphs** have doubled in size. They shed their skin once more and now look like proper spiders. The **egg sac** has become too small for them, so the mother makes a hole in it and the **spiderlings** escape.

Once they are outside, they gather around the sac for warmth and safety. They are hungry and need to find food. If they don't, they will start to eat each other.

The young spider finds food.

The young **spiderling** is the size of a pea. It is now able to catch and eat its own food.

At first, it eats small flies and insects. It catches its **prey** by jumping on it and biting it. Then it uses its hard, sharp **fangs** to inject **poison** into the animal, before sucking out the juices.

The spider makes a home.

When the **spiderling** moves away from the **egg sac**, it lives on its own. It will live alone until it mates. At first, it does not travel very far from its mother, but it must keep out of her way or she will eat it.

The young spider finds a piece of tree bark on the ground and looks for a small space in which to make its **burrow**. It lines its burrow with soft spider silk.

The spider catches its prey.

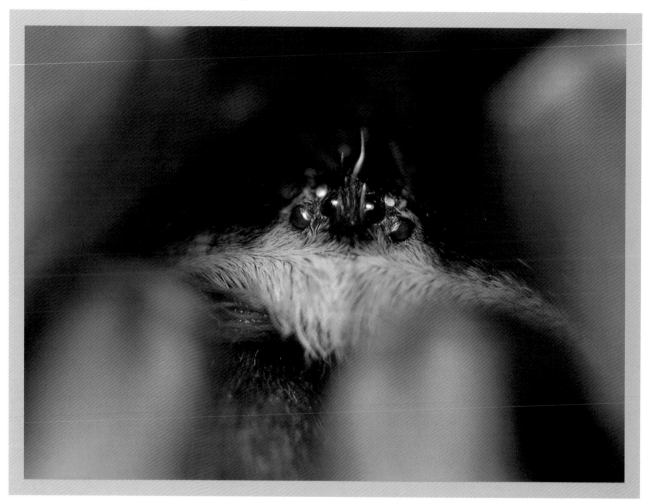

The spider has eight tiny eyes. They are the size of a pin tip. The eyes can only tell the difference between light and dark. The spider cannot use them to search for its **prey**.

The spider spins a fine cover of silk over the entrance to its **burrow**. It hides in the burrow until it feels an insect walking over the thin silk threads. Then it pounces on its prey.

The spider moults.

As it grows, the tarantula **moults**, or sheds, its skin. This happens every three months while it is young. Before it moults, it spins a thick bed of silk in its **burrow**.

It then turns around on the silk until it is upside down, then waits until it is ready to wriggle out. It pulls each leg out from the old skin, one by one, leaving its body until last. This takes about two days.

The spider is hairy.

The tarantula has a hairy body.
Some of the larger hairs are part of
the spider's senses. They can detect
the **vibrations** of moving **prey**.

Other hairs on the tarantula's back are shaped like tiny arrows. They sting if touched. If a **predator** gets too close, the spider rubs these hairs off and flicks them at its attacker.

The male looks for a mate.

A male tarantula takes at least three years to become an adult. During this time he lives alone in a **burrow** and feeds on passing insects.

When he is about three years old, the male leaves his home to search for a mate. When he finds a female spider, he drums his front legs on the ground to attract her. If she drums back, he knows he has been successful.

The male and female mate.

A female spider may sometimes attack a male, so he approaches her very slowly and carefully from the front. If the female is ready to mate, she will lift her front legs.

The male seizes her **fangs** with two hooks on his front legs so she cannot harm him. He places his **sperm** into the female, using his two **palps**. Afterwards, he leaves quickly before she can kill him.

The female makes her egg sac.

After the female tarantula has mated, she remains in her **burrow**. She does not have any eggs in her body yet. They develop over the next two or three months.

The female eats more food than usual to help the eggs grow. She weaves a silk cover and lays her eggs on it. She wraps the cover around them to make her **egg sac**.

Word bank

Burrow - Spiders live in burrows. These are hollows or holes that are built in a quiet or hidden place.

Egg sac - A sack that the spider spins from silk in order to protect the eggs.

Fangs - Sharp teeth at the front of the spider's mouth.

Moult - To shed or lose skin or hair.

Nymphs - Newly hatched spiders are called nymphs.

Palps - Two leg-like limbs that are attached to spiders' faces and enable them to mate. The male's palps are much larger than the female's.

Poison - A liquid or substance that causes death or illness to other living things.

Predators - Animals that hunt and eat other animals. A spider is a predator of small insects.

Prey - An animal that is or may be killed by another. Flies are the prey of spiders.

Sperm - Male cells needed to fertilise eggs.

Spiderlings - Baby spiders.

Spinnerets - An organ that enables the spider to spin their silk.

Vibrations - When something shakes or trembles it is vibrating.

Life cycle

A baby spider is growing inside each egg.

The female spider lays her eggs and wraps them in a silk egg sac.

After four weeks the eggs begin to change.

When a male is three years old he is fully grown. He mates with a female spider.

The baby spiders hatch and push themselves out of the shells.

The young spider makes its own burrow.

They grow in the egg sac for four weeks, shedding their skin twice.

They leave the egg sac and start to look for food.

Index